The Legend of the Peacock Princess

By Sunshine Orange Studio

Translated by Zhao Mingzhen

Adapted by Joe Gregory

Books Beyond Boundaries

ROYAL COLLINS

The Legend of the Peacock Princess

By Sunshine Orange Studio
Translated by Zhao Mingzhen
Adapted by Joe Gregory

First published in 2022 by Royal Collins Publishing Group Inc.
Groupe Publication Royal Collins Inc.
BKM Royalcollins Publishers Private Limited

Headquarters: 550-555 boul. René-Lévesque O Montréal (Québec) H2Z1B1 Canada
India office: 805 Hemkunt House, 8th Floor, Rajendra Place, New Delhi 110 008

Original Edition © Yunnan Education Publishing House Co., Ltd.

ISBN: 978-1-4878-1018-4

To find out more about our publications, please visit www.royalcollins.com.

Once upon a time, in the beautiful land of Xishuangbanna,
there lived a handsome prince in the Kingdom of Mengbanjia.
His name was Zhaoshutun.

Deep in the forest, there was also another kingdom called the Peacock Kingdom. In the Peacock Kingdom lived seven beautiful Peacock Princesses, each with a unique peacock-feather cape. When the princesses put their capes on, they would transform into beautiful peacocks, and they could fly freely in the air.

One day, Zhaoshutun got on his horse and went hunting in the deep forests as he often did. To his surprise, he saw the seven Peacock Princesses playing in a lake.

Zhaoshutun fell in love at first sight with the seventh and youngest princess, Nanmunuona, the most beautiful and intelligent of the seven Peacock Princesses.

Zhaoshutun did not want to let Nanmunuona leave, so he gingerly followed the legendary path and arrived at the lakeside. Then, he secretly took the peacock-feather cape that Nanmunuona had taken off and waited quietly in the forest.

When the Peacock Princesses were ready to put on their capes and fly away, they realized that the seventh princess Nanmunuona's cape had disappeared. At that moment, Zhaoshutun walked out of the woods, with Nanmunuona's cape in his hands.

When Nanmunuona saw the handsome prince, she fell in love with him, too.

Zhaoshutun apologized and expressed his love to Nanmunuona. At the same time, he asked the six sisters to help make the marriage succeed. From the bashful look on their sister's face, the six sisters understood that this was her wish too.

After expressing their blessings to the two lovers, the six Peacock Princesses put on their capes and flew away.

Zhaoshutun and Nanmunuona held a grand wedding ceremony, causing a great sensation throughout Mengbanjia. The old king of Mengbanjia, all his officials, and the common people blessed the couple. Their wedding ceremony lasted for three days and the water lamps of blessings filled the river.

After the marriage, Zhaoshutun and Nanmunuona lived happily together. But when neighboring tribes started a war, Zhaoshutun called on the bravest warriors in the Kingdom to protect their homeland. They all came on their elephants.

One day at the beginning of the war, came the bad news that Zhaoshutun's army had been defeated and forced to retreat. The war was getting closer to Mengbanjia. The old king became desperate and believed the false charge that the war had been brought to the country by Nanmunuona, so he decided to burn her to death.

Right before her execution, Nanmunuona asked to put on her peacock-feather cape one last time, so she could give her father one last peacock dance, thanking the people for their love towards her.

The old king agreed. Nanmunuona put on her peacock-feather cape and danced the peacock dance, full of love for Zhaoshutun and the people of Mengbanjia.

At the end of the dance, Nanmunuona turned
into a colorful peacock, and with pitiful eyes,
she slowly flew up and away into the sky.

The news of the prince's victory arrived on the evening of the same day. But when Zhaoshutun could not find his wife in the crowd that welcomed the triumphant return of the army, he started to worry.

Back with the old king, Zhaoshutun explained what had happened. Nanmunuona had come up with the plan to lure the enemy closer and closer, lulling them into a false sense of security. When the time was ripe, Mengbanjia attacked and was able to win the war!

Hearing this, the old king was full of regret, but it was already too late. He told Zhaoshutun what had happened to Nanmunuona, and how he had forced her to leave.

When Zhaoshutun heard what had happened, he was distraught and set off on his horse. The only thing he could think about was that he needed to find his wife. But how would he find the legendary Peacock Kingdom in the dense forests? He started calling out for his wife, shouting at the top of his lungs.

Then, a miracle happened: a holy monkey appeared before his eyes! The monkey handed Nanmunuona's bracelet to Zhaoshutun, and also gave him three magical gold arrows and a bow that she had left. Finally, the monkey directed Zhaoshutun toward the Peacock Kingdom.

After Zhaoshutun had crossed many mountains, the holy monkey told him to use one of the gold arrows to shoot open the mountain blocking the way to the Peacock Kingdom. He did this and a road leading to the Peacock Kingdom appeared.

After the long and hard journey, Zhaoshutun was forced to use his second gold arrow to kill the Devil Snake blocking the way. Zhaoshutun and the holy monkey had suffered serious wounds, but they finally reached the homeland of the Peacock Princesses.

Since the youngest daughter had been treated unfairly in Mengbanjia, the king of the Peacock Kingdom decided to test whether Zhaoshutun could protect his daughter. If not, the king would not let her go.

The king asked his seven daughters to stand behind a gauze curtain, each with a candle on her head. He asked Zhaoshutun to find his wife among the seven princesses and use his bow and arrow to put out the candle on his wife's head.

Zhaoshutun steadied himself and he took out the third and last gold arrow. The magic arrow hit the candle on the head of Nanmunuona. The gauze curtain fell, revealing the graceful Nanmunuona, lovingly gazing at her husband.

At last, Zhaoshutun found his wife and after the hardship they had both gone through, their love for each other was deeper than ever.

Ever since then, the Dai people in Mengbanjia have had a special relationship to the peacock, which is regarded as a symbol of good luck and happiness. The peacock dance, symbolizing peace and happiness, also has a special place in the hearts of the people.